NO

The Apostle
of Peace

Abbot Martin Geudens

*All booklets are published
thanks to the generosity of the supporters
of the Catholic Truth Society*

All rights reserved. First published 2020 by The Incorporated Catholic Truth Society, 42-46 Harleyford Road, London SE11 5AY. Tel: 020 7640 0042 Fax: 020 7640 0046. © 2020 The Incorporated Catholic Truth Society. www.ctsbooks.org

ISBN 978 1 78469 630 6

Contents

His Early Life and Conversion

The twelfth century witnessed troubles which divided Europe, and even schisms and divisions which divided the Church. During this chaos, Divine Providence raised up St Norbert as an apostle of peace, an apostle of the Blessed Sacrament, a strong defender of the Church, and as the founder of a new Order.

Norbert was born around the year 1080 at Xanten, a town in Westphalia in Germany. His father, Heribert, Count of Gennep, was related to the imperial house of Germany, and his mother, Hedwig of Guise, was a descendant of the ancient House of Lorraine.

Norbert was endowed with great spiritual and natural gifts. It was said that, "In health he was robust, in stature tall, in bearing graceful and refined, quick and penetrating of intellect, tractable and tender of heart."

Norbert was ordained subdeacon and appointed to a canonry in the church at Xanten. His archbishop, having heard of his great learning and natural talents, placed him in his court at Cologne.

As a young man, Norbert allowed himself to be carried away by the pleasures of life. Being ambitious and fond of honours, he succeeded in obtaining a second ecclesiastical preferment – a canonry at Cologne cathedral – besides other church dignities. All this, however, did not satisfy his ambitions. He left the archiepiscopal court of Cologne and joined the court of Emperor Henry V where he was appointed chaplain and almoner.

In this capacity he was present at all the imperial diets and was chosen to accompany the Emperor to Rome. The Emperor wanted to make peace with Pope Paschal II and to receive the imperial crown from the hands of His Holiness. The negotiations were, however, soon broken off, and the Emperor endeavoured to obtain by force that which he could not by peaceful means. He ordered his army to Rome, and the Pope was made a prisoner. Norbert was scandalised by this act against the Church. He visited the Pope in prison and consoled him in his distress. Sadly, Norbert was still too ambitious, too much of a courtier, to listen to the voice of his conscience and to leave the Emperor.

Norbert's Conversion

After this, the Bishopric of Cambrai was offered to Norbert by the Emperor, but Norbert, afraid of the Church's condemnation despite his own ambition, refused the dignity. Yet, so thoroughly was he enslaved to the world, nothing short of a miracle of grace could change this ambitious Saul into another Paul. This needed miracle of grace soon changed Norbert's life forever.

Norbert was riding one day, attended by only one servant, when he was suddenly overtaken by a violent thunderstorm. The servant, overcome with fear, exclaimed, "Where are you going? Come back, for the hand of God is against you." Hardly had he uttered these prophetic words, when, with a loud clap of thunder, lightning fell at the horse's feet, burning the grass and tearing up the earth. The horse threw off its rider, who lay like one dead for nearly an hour. Coming to himself, he cried to God in his heart, "Lord, what would you have me do?" To this question Divine Grace replied, "Turn away from evil, and do good; seek after peace, and pursue it."

Norbert became on the spot a sincere penitent. Renouncing his appointments at court, he returned to Xanten, where he led a life of penance, and spent his time in tears and prayers. He placed himself entirely under the direction of Conon, the holy Abbot of Siburg, and led a monastic life without becoming a monk.

His soul, burning with apostolic zeal, placed no limits to his penance and he aspired simply to serve him whom he had so long disregarded. Norbert was now thirty-five years old.

Norbert's Ordination and Zeal

Norbert felt called to the priesthood, even though believing himself unworthy of it. In his zeal to serve God and reform his life, he asked the archbishop if he could be ordained a deacon and a priest on the same day.

This unusual request greatly surprised the archbishop, who knew the worldly life that Norbert had led, but he consented to comply with his wishes.

It was after fervent preparation that Norbert, on Holy Saturday 1115, entered the cathedral church of Cologne. Desiring to make reparation for the scandals he had given, he threw off his princely garments and appeared clothed in sheepskin, with a cord around his waist. Over this he put the sacred vestments. Dressed like a penitent, he received Holy Orders from the hands of the archbishop.

After his ordination he returned to Abbot Conon, and under his direction made a retreat of forty days, fasting each day on bread and water and studying the duties of his sacred ministry.

On leaving the guidance of the holy abbot, he returned to Xanten, where he celebrated his first Mass in the presence of the canons and a great number of people.

After the gospel had been sung, Norbert, turned to the people and preached on the fleeting pleasures of this world, on the emptiness of its honours and promises.

At a chapter (the name for a meeting of the canons) held on the following day, he spoke to the canons of their great want of discipline and with great passion he urged them to reform their lives. The older canons were deeply moved and looked upon Norbert as one sent from heaven to restore monastic discipline. However, the younger canons were unwilling to change and were so angered at hearing their lives exposed that they left the chapter house.

Norbert, in no way offended by this insult, still persevered, in season and out of season, to bring them back to a better discipline. The younger canons were more bitter than before; a young cleric insulted him, spat on his face, and would have done more, had he not been prevented by other clerics. Norbert excused the young cleric, and thanked God for this occasion of doing penance for his former sins.

The Abbey of Kloosterrath

At this time, Norbert often went to the Abbey of Siburg to confer with Abbot Conon, his spiritual director, or to the cell of Ludolph, a holy hermit whose close friend he was, or to the Abbey of Kloosterrath, near Rolduc and not far from Xanten.

It was in the Abbey of Kloosterrath that Norbert manifested the liveliness and fervour of his faith and deep reverence for the Blessed Sacrament. As Norbert was saying Mass, at the consecration of the chalice, a large spider fell into the Precious Blood. At that time, many believed all spiders to be poisonous. (In Shakespeare, for example, we read "adders, spiders, toads, or any creeping venom'd thing that lives" (*Richard III*, i: 2) and – "there may be in the cup a spider steep'd" (*The Winters Tale* ii: 1).

Such was the fervour of Norbert's Faith, such was his reverence for the Precious Blood, that at the Communion of the Mass he received the Precious Blood containing the spider and prepared to die at the foot of the altar. In prayer and in contemplating his death, he suddenly sneezed and was 'relieved' of the spider. It is a great witness to Norbert's intense love and respect for the Blessed Sacrament that he was prepared to die rather than dishonour the Precious Blood.

The contemporary author of *The Life of St Norbert* (Vita B) says that this incident shows in the clearest manner how lively his faith in God was. "Two virtues" he says, "were necessary for him to do the work which God had destined for him – the virtues of patience and faith." Patience served him for a shield; faith gave him strength. "So great was his faith," he continues, "that by common consent he was said to possess it to the highest degree." Faith was deemed to be his characteristic virtue.

11

At that time, it was a common saying that faith excelled in Norbert, charity in Bernard of Clairvaux and humility in Milo, Bishop of Thérouanne.

Norbert at the Council of Fritzlar, Visiting the Pope and his Missionary Journey

Norbert's enemies endeavoured to discredit him in the eyes of the ecclesiastical authorities. The legate of Pope Gelasius II had at that time assembled a council at Fritzlar for the maintenance of the Pope's authority in Germany. To this council Norbert was summoned and was accused of being a hypocrite and one who cloaked evil designs under the pretext of zeal for a reformation of morals. Norbert, remembering the sins of his past life, confessed that he deserved all manner of contempt and ill treatment. Nevertheless, he cleared himself of all their calumnies. The Pope's legate could easily see that the only motive for these accusations was to be found in Norbert's virtuous life, and in his zeal to reform the clergy. Yet, fearing he would alienate the good will of the bishops and other dignitaries present, the legate made no decision and allowed Norbert to leave the council.

Persecuted on all sides, misunderstood and deserted by his friends, Norbert sought consolation at the foot of the cross, and spent many hours in fervent prayer. He left Fritzlar and went to Cologne where he resigned all his ecclesiastical preferments. He sold his estate, and distributed the money amongst the poor, keeping only a mule and the sacred vestments necessary for Mass. He dismissed all his servants except for two who begged to be allowed to remain with him.

Barefooted and begging his bread, he journeyed onward till he reached the town of St Giles, in Languedoc, France. There Pope Gelasius was holding his pontifical court, having been compelled to leave Rome by the persecution of the Emperor Henry.

Meeting the Holy Father

On his arrival Norbert threw himself at the feet of the Holy Father, begging absolution of all his past sins, especially of the irregularities committed by him in receiving the Holy Orders of deacon and priest on the same day, without having observed the interval of time mandated by the Church.

Pope Gelasius was greatly impressed by Norbert and desired to keep him at his court. Norbert, who trembled at the very thought of resuming the life of a courtier, asked the Pope's permission to leave and his blessing to preach the gospel of Christ. As Pope Gelasius was unable to retain him at his side, he gave him full faculties to preach wherever he judged proper.

It was then the depth of winter, yet Norbert walked barefooted through the snow. His entire life was a

14

continual Lent. He never took meals until evening, except
on Sundays. He passed his days in preaching and his nights
in prayer.

Passing through Orleans in the beginning of Lent 1118,
he was joined by a subdeacon who asked to remain with
him and to assist him in his missionary work.

Norbert, with his two former servants who had become
colleagues and the young subdeacon, journeyed as far
as Valenciennes, where they arrived on the eve of Palm
Sunday. Not being able to address the people in their own
language, he prayed for their welfare. During his prayer
it came to his mind that the Holy Spirit had bestowed on
the apostles the gift of languages; he asked for the sake of
apostolate and for the benefit of the town that the people
might understand what he should say to them in German.

Full of faith and confidence in God's mercies, he
mounted the pulpit and preached in his own language and
was understood by the people as if he had spoken to them
in their own language. This wonderful event caused many
conversions in the town.

However, such were the rigours of their penances, that
his three disciples fell ill and died. Their death cost Norbert
many tears, but God soon consoled him in his sorrow.

Bishop of Cambrai

Burchard, Bishop of Cambrai, had at that time arrived at
Valenciennes. Norbert knew him at the Emperor's court,

and he went to visit his former friend but was not at first recognised by him. After a few moments, Burchard realised who he was and exclaimed, "O Norbert! Who could have believed in such a change! Are you the noble prince whose glory and riches all admired?"

The tears and the marks of tender friendship astonished Hugh, the bishop's chaplain, who was present but who did not understand the German which they spoke together. When the bishop had explained to him who Norbert was, Hugh was so deeply touched that he asked permission to accompany Norbert and to assist him in his apostolic labours. This great man became Norbert's first disciple and afterwards, when Norbert was raised to the see of Magdeburg, he succeeded him in government of the Order.

Now accompanied by Hugh, Norbert preached penance in Hainault, Brabant and Liège. The people crowded to hear him and wherever he went his sermons, strengthened by the example of an evangelical life, produced the conversion of hardened sinners and reconciled many.

The great zeal which Norbert had for the salvation of souls did not make him forget the spiritual education of Hugh, his disciple. Any spare moments that he could find were spent in this important work. He urged him to practise the virtues of patience, humility and poverty.

My brother let this virtue of poverty not discourage you; Jesus Christ has borne all the burden of it; be not disheartened but embrace what your redeemer first practised. St Laurence poured the treasures of the Church into the hands of the poor; imitate his example in the disposal of your property. This generous sacrifice which I advise you to make is not according to the liking of a covetous heart, but the spirit of poverty is necessary in order to preach the gospel. Be not ashamed of humiliations; they are the germ of glory. Be attentive to the custody of your chastity; this virtue will transform you into an angel. Be prompt to comply with the orders of obedience; it is by this virtue that you will raise yourself to an understanding of God's greatness. Arm yourself with patience in adversities; they are the portion of the elect. Do not expect a better lot than that of the apostles: you are heir to their ministry; you will be heir to their sufferings.

Norbert, the Apostle of Peace

Having left the diocese of Cambrai, Norbert preached in Liège, and commenced his missionary work at Fosse.

His austere life and the success of his preaching were already known there and both clergy and laity crowded to hear him. They requested his help to reconcile two families which had long been divided by a deadly hatred. More than sixty people had been murdered in consequence of this family feud.

While they were still entreating Norbert to restore peace, the brother of someone who had been killed by the opposing family arrived. Norbert embraced the young man and said, "My dear friend, I a stranger in this place, a mere passer-by, entreat you to forgive the murderer of your brother; God will give you the reward." The young man, touched by his genuine words, promised to forgive the murderer and to put an end to hateful feuds.

On the following Saturday a meeting of the two hostile families was to be held. Norbert prepared himself for it by long and fervent prayers and acts of penance.

When Norbert had finished his preparation, he said first one Mass in honour of Our Lady, then another for the souls of those whose death had been caused by this feud. When the second Mass was ended, he mounted the pulpit and he preached on peace. The people were so deeply impressed by what Norbert said about peace that both parties agreed to put their cause in his hands, and they swore lasting peace.

The New Pope

From Fosse Norbert went to Gemblours, a small town in Brabant, where the astonished crowds hailed him as an angel of peace. Here Norbert endeavoured to reconcile two other deadly foes. One was willing to be reconciled, but the other would not listen to Norbert and rejected his message of peace. This unfortunate man was that same week struck dead by his enemy.

While Norbert was still in Belgium on his mission of peace, he learnt that Pope Calixtus II has succeeded Gelasius and that a council had been convoked for the 21st October at Rheims. He travelled to the city to ask the Holy Father for a renewal of the faculties which had been granted by his predecessor. Being unable to obtain an audience with the Pope, he and his disciples left Rheims and stayed to rest on the road near the Abbey of St Thierry in the hope that eventually they would be allowed to see the Pope.

Bartholomew, Bishop of Laon, happened to pass by the road. This prelate noticed three pilgrim strangers and asked the reason for their journey. Norbert replied that they had been to Rheims in order to obtain of the new Pope a renewal of the faculties granted by his predecessor, but that, sadly, after waiting three days for an audience, they had met with refusal.

The bishop, touched by this encounter, requested them to return with him, and promised to speak on their behalf with Pope Calixtus and to obtain an audience for them. From Hugh, the bishop learnt all about Norbert's noble birth and manner of life. He was so edified with the account that at his first audience he gave a full account of it to the Pope, to whom he also introduced Norbert. Norbert appeared before the Pope in his penitential dress. He gave an account of the result of his missionary labours and obtained the Pope's blessing and fresh grant of faculties like those which he had received from Pope Gelasius.

Return to Laon

The council ended and the Pope asked Norbert to accompany Bishop Bartholomew and return with him to Laon where the Pope had decided to remain during the winter. Norbert's biographer says that, "as soon as Pope Calixtus had arrived, the Pope and bishop both deliberated how they could best retain the man of God in the diocese". "It was at their suggestion", he writes, "that the canons at St Martin at Laon elected Norbert as their abbot, for there were great abuses in the abbey, which the Pope wished to see reformed." To the Pope, Norbert replied,

O Father, you remember that I have twice been commissioned to preach the Word of God, first by authority of your predecessor and then by you. However, I do not wish to follow my own will, I am ready to undertake the responsibility... but I will state in short that I have chosen to lead a strictly evangelical and apostolic life. I do not refuse the burden, if the canons are willing to follow this rule of life.

The Pope answered that if the canons could not be reformed, Norbert was free to leave them.

At his first sermon at St Martin's, Norbert explained to the canons that those who wish to follow Christ must patiently suffer hunger and thirst, reproach and calumny and in obedience observe the rules of the Fathers. On hearing this the canons expressed their outrage at Norbert. They did not wish to change their manner of living and they would not submit to his rules and regulations, which they considered too severe. Norbert, very happily, resigned his new post with a clear conscience.

Norbert and Prémontré

Norbert, relieved of the government of the canons of St Martin, remained at the bishop's palace. Bartholomew wanted Norbert to found a religious house in his diocese.

Norbert consented and the bishop accompanied him to find a spot favourable for a conventual life. They visited various places, but none of them seemed right to Norbert. Finally, Bartholomew led him far into the forest of Coucy, where they found a deep marshy valley named Prémontré, where the waters congregated from the high mountains, and the ground was covered with thorns and brushwood. There was a little chapel, dedicated to St John the Baptist, which had fallen into ruin. Into this chapel they entered to pray. Norbert, being immediately seized with the Spirit of God, begged to be allowed to remain all night in prayer.

Whilst Norbert was praying most fervently that God would direct him in founding his Order, the Queen of Angels appeared to him and told him that his prayers were granted. She indicated that this was the place where he should build the first house of the Order, and she gave him the white habit of the Order, saying "Receive, my Son, the white habit." After this the Queen of Heaven disappeared, and Norbert remained enraptured in prayer.

Norbert, radiant with joy, exclaimed,

This is the place of my rest and haven of my salvation. Here I must sing the praises of the Lord together with faithful companions, whom the Lord will send to proclaim his mercies. This chapel, however, shall not be the principal church of the monastery; another will be built at the other side of the mountain. I have seen during my prayer a multitude of pilgrims, clothed in white robes, carrying in their hands crosses and censers, who pointed out the place where God wished to have a church erected in his honour.

Winter at Prémontré

An Order, which should have penance for its portion and preaching for its occupation, could only take its birth in solitude dedicated to St John the Baptist, the model preacher of penance.

Bartholomew, satisfied with Norbert's choice, procured for him the possession of Prémontré. Norbert took possession of his dear solitude in 1120. Bartholomew, for his part, never ceased to provide for the support of Norbert and his companions.

Soon after, preaching at Laon, Norbert so touched the hearts of seven young men – all sons of the best families of Lorraine – that they followed him to Prémontré and became his disciples.

He remained all the winter at Prémontré, watching over and instructing his young community. In the beginning of spring he left it to the care of Hugh, and went to Cambrai, where he gained another new disciple, Evermode, already well-known for his learning and piety, who later became Bishop of Ratzburg. Many followed his example, so that before the end of Lent Norbert returned to Prémontré accompanied by thirteen new disciples.

In the absence of the founder, an evil spirit had caused a disturbance among the community. When Norbert had reached the valley of Prémontré, he was caught in a storm during which God revealed to the saint the pitiful state of the young community. A young religious named Gerard, who had been a model of piety and obedience, had listened to the suggestions of Satan and had publicly broken his Lenten fast and abstinence. Norbert embraced him with the affection of a father but punished him with the severity of a judge. Gerard willingly accepted the penances, so that he became afterwards a model of virtue. During the remaining days of Lent, Norbert instructed his brothers and encouraged them, especially in the practice of patience.

Norbert and the Early Months of the Order of Prémontré

Toward the end of April Norbert returned to Nivelles where, owing to some of his disciples having left Prémontré and spoken ill of him and his Order, he found the people hostile to him. These calumnies the saint bore with great patience and the calumniators were soon brought to shame. During his stay in the town, a young girl possessed by the devil was brought to Norbert and he expelled the unclean spirit during the Holy Sacrifice of the Mass. He restored the girl to her parents who were full of gratitude to him, and the people proclaimed afresh his holiness of life.

Norbert then travelled to Cologne, so that he might secure in this resting place of the remains of so many saints, relics of some martyrs for the new church at Prémontré.

The Archbishop of Cologne was delighted to see Norbert and granted his request. The burial place of St Ursula, unknown for centuries, was indicated in an apparition to Norbert. In a similar manner, the relics of St Gereon and his companions were discovered.

Towards the end of October, he returned to Prémontré, with a portion of these relics, and accompanied by new disciples. Their journey was a succession of miracles, for wherever the relics rested, God poured out his blessing. The Countess of Namur was so much struck during a conversation which she had with Norbert that she offered him her manor house of Floreffe that he might establish an abbey there. Norbert accepted the offer and appointed Blessed Richard the first abbot. After a short stay at Floreffe, Norbert continued his journey in order to be at Prémontré for the feast of Christmas, to receive on that day the profession of the brethren.

They had lived so far without a written rule. They wished to lead an apostolic life, but they were not bound by any permanent obligation. Charity was the bond of their association and the example of their master served as their rule of life.

Christ Crucified

Norbert spoke about this to his disciples. He said that he had consulted learned bishops and holy abbots; by some he was advised to lead an eremitical life, by others a monastic life, or else to join the Cistercian Order. However, he preferred the canonical life of the apostles, but they must know the Will of God. He asked them to increase their prayers and mortifications so as to implore the light of the Holy Spirit.

It was at that time that St Augustine appeared to him and gave him his rule in these words: "I am Augustine,

Bishop of Hippo. Behold, here you have now a rule which I have written; if your fellow brethren my sons shall have observed it well, they shall stand without fear in the presence of Christ at the terrible last day of Judgement."

Norbert then composed the form of their vows which all pronounced on the solemn feast of Christmas 1121. So began the Order of Canons Regular of Prémontré.

On the spot where the church was built at Prémontré, Christ crucified appeared to Hugh, St Norbert's first disciple. Seven sunbeams of great brightness shone upon our crucified Redeemer and a multitude of white robed pilgrims holding staffs in their hands, coming from the four quarters of the world, paid homage to the cross on their knees, kissed the feet of their saviour and then returned to preach the name of Christ crucified.

History has proved the truth of this prophecy, for the Order – to quote the words of Pope Adrian IV – was "rich in glory and merits extended its branches from sea to sea, like a prolific vine."

After this glorious beginning, Norbert continued to encourage the brethren and he never tired of recommending to them his three favourite maxims.

The first was cleanliness, that should be observed about the altar and in the celebration of the sacred mysteries; for on the altar, as he said, we prove the liveliness of our faith and the fervour of our love. Secondly, confession in the chapter house of all their faults and negligences, for this confession will render their consciences purer, and their watchfulness greater. Thirdly, love for the poor and hospitality towards their neighbour; for a house where these three maxims are strictly observed will never be in want.

Alongside the many men who joined Prémontré, the Lord called an equal number of women to join the Order. Notable among them was Blessed Ricvera, St Norbert's first spiritual daughter. Her example was followed by many others including Anastasia, Duchess of Pomerania, Hedwig, Countess of Cleves, Adelia of Montmorency, daughter of Burchard, constable of France, and St Gertrude, daughter of St Elizabeth of Hungary. Thousands of women chose the white habit with the black veil of penance in the Order of Prémontré. Their number increased to such an extent that in less than fifteen years there were more than ten thousand canonesses of the Order in the various countries of Europe.

Norbert Against the Devil, Founding of the Third Order and His Success at Antwerp

The holy lives of Norbert and his disciples roused more than ever the anger of Satan, who, when Norbert was away from Prémontré, never ceased in his endeavours to attack his community.

Sometimes the devils seemed to attack Prémontré with a tumult of soldiers assaulting a stronghold, when cries are heard of victors and vanquished. Hugh dispersed the enemies with the sign of the cross. At the name of Norbert, the devils trembled and were silent. One of them took possession of the body of a lay brother, and having confessed that he was the same evil spirit whom Norbert – called by the devils "that white dog, whose birth may be cursed forever" – had expelled from a girl at Nivelles, the lay brother was exorcised and the devil was forced to abandon his victim.

Whilst all this was taking place at Prémontré, Norbert went from town to town, preaching penance to sinners, healing the sick, delivering those that were possessed, converting the hard of heart, and comforting the just.

Norbert crossed the Rhine and preached in Westphalia. Among those who first yielded to the influence of his holy example was Godfrey, Count of Cappenberg, who offered his castle to Norbert, so that it might be turned into an abbey. The fame of Godfrey's conversion soon spread throughout Westphalia.

Theobald, Count of Champagne, had heard of Norbert's fame and wanted to meet him. This nobleman, surnamed the Great, was son of Stephen, Count of Champagne, and Alice, daughter of William the Conqueror, King of England. He succeeded to the princely estates in 1102 and was said to own as many castles as there are days in the year.

On Norbert's return to France from Westphalia, Theobald met him, and expressed his earnest wish to join his Order. Norbert, after long prayer and mature consideration, explained to Theobald that he was called to serve God in the state of matrimony and that he would be blessed with numerous offspring to inherit his property and so maintain the needs of the general population.

Theobald humbly submitted to this decision. He asked Norbert to give him a rule of life which he might observe in the world, in order to live like a member of the Order of Prémontré. Norbert vested him with the white scapular, which Theobald wore underneath his secular clothes. It was in this way that the Third Order of Prémontré was instituted for the benefit of people living in the world, so that they might share in the prayers and good works of the entire Order. Pope Benedict XIV confirmed that it is the oldest "third Order" in the Church, a fact restated by

Pope Pius XI in his brief "Antiquis Monasteriis" (1921), which states that, "Among [the] groups of Tertiaries [in the Church], that one must be considered the oldest which flourished in the Order of Canons Regular of Prémontré, and rejoices in having St Norbert, the founder of the Order, as their founder."

Defending the Truth of the Catholic Faith

Shortly after this, Norbert was called to Antwerp. That city had become the headquarters of the heretic Tanchelin.

It was said that Tanchelin had united in the same sect the abominations of the Gnostics, the heresies of Berengar of Tours, the errors of the Donatists and the idolatry of the Simonians. He openly asserted that the priesthood was a fiction, and that the Holy Eucharist and the other sacraments were empty and of no value. He had already spread his errors throughout Holland, Flanders and the territory of Antwerp. At the head of three thousand fanatical disciples, he committed the most terrible crimes everywhere. The Bishop of Cambrai had sent twelve secular canons to Antwerp to counter this heresy, but they found the evils too deeply rooted to be eradicated by them. The bishop implored the assistance of Norbert, whose sanctity and erudition were widely known.

Accompanied by Evermode, Waltman and several others, these defenders of the truth of the Catholic Faith made their way to Antwerp. Addressing the people who had assembled to hear him, he said, "I am aware that the ignorance of truth, rather than the love of error, is the principal cause of your forsaking the one true religion." In his addresses to the people, he combined the gentleness of persuasion with the force of sound arguments. The success of his mission was such that in a short time the people perceived their errors, souls were converted and abuses reformed.

The bishop rejoiced at this happy change and entreated the founder of Prémontré to accept a church and establish a house of the Order in Antwerp. Norbert accepted the offer, and founded the Abbey of St Michael, and installed Blessed Waltman as its first abbot.

The Spread of the Order of Prémontré

The news of Norbert's success over the heresy at Antwerp soon spread throughout Europe, and people spoke of his zeal, his kindness, his holiness and his learning.

The Order grew rapidly. Each day brought new postulants to Prémontré. The Order had existed but three years, and though numbering already several abbeys and hundreds of religious, it had only been approved by bishops. For a more solemn confirmation, Norbert petitioned the Pope's legates, Peter di Leone and Gregory de Angelis, to confirm in the Pope's name the Order which had been established at Prémontré. The legates were very happy to do this:

> Peter di Leone, priest, and Gregory de Angelis, deacon, cardinals and legates of the Holy See, to our venerable brother Norbert, and to all his brethren who profess under him the canonical life, health and benediction. We give thanks to Almighty God – whose mercy is of greater value than our lives – because you renew the praiseworthy lives of the Holy Fathers, and under the inspirations of the Holy Spirit raise up the institutions founded from the commencement of the

Church, on the teaching of the apostles, which are nearly extinguished. For there were in the beginning of the Church two conditions of life instituted for her children: the one for the weak, the other for the strong; the one remaining in small Segor, the other ascending the summit of high mountains; the one redeeming sins by penance and alms, the other by the daily practice of virtues acquiring eternal merits; the one engaged in the world, possesses worldly goods; the other, raised on high, despises and forsakes them. But the kind of life which by divine fervour is disengaged from earthly desires is subdivided into two classes aiming at nearly the same end, namely into those of canons and those of monks. The latter (that of monks), has, by God's mercy, always been conspicuous by the number of those who professed it. The former (that of canons) which, with the charity of the faithful becoming cold, was nearly extinguished, begins by God's mercy to acquire new life and vigour. St Urban, Pope and martyr, instituted it; St Augustine gave it his rule; St Jerome reformed it. We should therefore deem it not a less meritorious work to re-establish under God's inspiration, and with his grace, the canonical life, so well-known in the primitive Church, than to preserve the monastic life, which is kept in its vigour by the same grace of God. Therefore, we confirm by the authority of the Holy See, whose legates we are, your state of life, and in the name of God we exhort and beseech you to persevere in it. We also grant, to those who profess the canonical life in your monasteries, the blessing of the holy apostles Ss Peter and Paul, and the pardon of all their sins. We direct that no one be allowed to change the state of your Order, the benefits of which have been shared by so many countries, in order that many more may obtain the blessing of your ministrations. We also decree that no member of your Order from lightness of character, or under pretence of a more austere life, be allowed to leave your Order for another, without the consent of the abbot and of the whole community, and we prohibit any abbot or bishop to receive him without the necessary testimonials as to this consent. You, therefore, dearest brethren in Christ, endeavour with renewed zeal to fulfil most faithfully what you have promised. "Let your light shine before men, that they may see your good works, and glorify your Father who is in heaven." It is in the Name of the Father and of His Son and of the Holy Spirit, that we confirm what we now decree. Should anyone after two or three warnings act against these decrees, let him be banished according to the canonical penalties. I, Peter di Leone, priest and Legate of the Holy See; I, Gregory de Angelis, Cardinal Deacon and Legate of the Holy See. Given at Noyen, 28th June 1124, the sixth of the pontificate of Pope Calixtus II.

Norbert's Apostolic Journeys and Return to Prémontré

Meanwhile, Norbert, having thus completed the great work of establishing his Order, went to Germany to conclude a treaty of marriage between Theobald (the first member of the Third Order) and Maud, daughter of the Marquess of Crayburg.

Having reached Germany, Norbert decided on a journey to Rome, so he remained at Regensburg till spring would allow him to set out for the Eternal City.

Pope Honorius II had succeeded Calixtus II more than a year before. Having heard so much good of Norbert and his Order, the Pope received him at Rome and again confirmed the Order of Prémontré by a bull, dated Rome, 27th February 1126.

After receiving the Pope's blessing, Norbert left Rome and commenced his journey home by way of Germany. Despite the difficulties of the journey, he observed the strict rules of Lent, and preached in the several towns through which he and his companions passed.

At Würzburg, clergy as well as laity came out to meet him and desired him to preach and sing Mass on Easter

Sunday. Whilst our saint was singing High Mass on Easter Sunday, a blind woman asked to be carried before the altar, and at Communion she entreated him to restore her sight. Norbert, touched with compassion and seeing her faith, breathed on the eyes of the blind woman, and to the great astonishment of all present, she instantly recovered the use of her eyes.

On leaving Germany, Norbert hastened to return to Prémontré, where he arrived at the end of May after an absence of six months.

Satan had continued his endeavours to destroy the work which Norbert had so happily begun for the glory of God and the salvation of souls. At Prémontré, their sleep was almost nightly disturbed by violent shaking of the walls of the monastery, or by forms of the most hideous creatures. The wicked enemy, however, was always overcome and put to shame.

Whilst Norbert was engaged in prayer, Satan appeared in the shape of a bear, with its mouth wide open and its claws stretched out. Norbert made the sign of the cross and said,

What are you waiting for? Your claws are useless, your horrible teeth are but wind, and your shaggy coat is but mist and smoke, which vanish before the rays of the sun. In your creation you were light, but by your pride you have deserved darkness. Begone, I command you, because there is no concord between Christ and

Beelzebub, no share of the faithful with unbelievers. Make haste and depart. You know that you can do no harm."

At these words, the devil disappeared.

Norbert's Spiritual Testament

Theobald, count of Champagne, again needed the help of Norbert. The Count requested that he accompany him to conclude the final negotiations for his intended marriage. Norbert could not refuse the count's request. Before leaving Prémontré, he called his religious together, and addressed them. These words form Norbert's spiritual testament to his beloved children:

We exhort you, dearest brethren, to be most diligent in the service of God, to whom you have consecrated yourselves by solemn profession of your vows. For, having by your own free will and from pure love of God renounced your earthly possessions and even yourselves, you are obliged daily to carry the cross of Christ; that is, you are obliged continually to mortify your passions and to spend your whole life in works of penance.

This is, indeed, the narrow road to heaven. This is the road which Jesus Christ has pointed out beforehand, both by his life and death, by his words and deeds, and which leads to our heavenly country all those who to the end of their lives walk in that path. You cannot go to Christ unless you enter upon this narrow road with courage and confidence and do your best to follow it; for the apostle St Paul has said, "None is crowned except he strive lawfully." (*2 Tm* 2:5) and St John, "who abides in Christ, ought himself also to walk, even as he walked." (*1 Jn* 2:6).

Walk therefore cautiously in the way which God has shown you, lest you be overtaken by an unlooked-for death. Let your obedience be prompt, your poverty voluntary, and your chastity above suspicion; without these three virtues that which constitutes an Order is wholly destroyed.

You have promised stability or perseverance in this holy place; remain, therefore, faithful in the service of God, and never grow weary of your duties in the monastery. Never leave it except when you are occasionally obliged to do so on account of temporal affairs, lest these useless excursions rob you of the sweetness of a virtuous life, and of the consolation which you find in the contemplation of the divine mysteries; and lest also these excursions lead you astray and cause you to love this wicked world, wherein there is no place free from corruption. For, as a fish out of water is entirely deprived of its natural and necessary element and hence soon dies, so a vagrant religious frequently found in the midst of a wicked world, deprived as he is of the protection of his cloister, far away from the example and salutary lessons of his brethren, soon falls into sin and gets entangled in the snares of everlasting death. Flee, therefore, my dearest brethren, the company of worldly persons, as a fish avoids a dry place, but love the cloister, which protects you and which keeps the mind pure; for you make an unworthy use of the glorious name of your religious vocation if by your earthly desires you show that you are more attached to the world than to God.

Remain, therefore, constantly in the monastery, and remain there united in the bonds of charity. Keep a watch over your tongue, in order that by avoiding murmuring, detraction and envy, you may dwell together in the house of God in peace and concord; for a slanderous and deceitful tongue is a restless evil and is full of deadly poison. It never ceases to do harm; it destroys the advantages of peace and makes one less devoted to religion. It is therefore written of such, "A quarrelsome and grumbling monk is never a true monk."

Wherefore, put restraint on your tongue. Raise up your hearts to the kingdom of heaven, where true joys are to be found. Raised up by holy desires, take your flight with the saints in the regions above, in the contemplation of the divine mysteries. Bear with grief the burden of your bodies, so that you may say with the apostle "I desire to be dissolved and to be with Christ." (*Ph* 1:23). And with the psalmist "Bring our souls out of the prisons of our bodies" (*Ps* 141), that you may reign with Christ forever and ever.

Though outwardly fairly clad with the white habit – a symbol of simplicity and innocence – but outwardly miserably deprived of the spirit of religious perfection, should any of you not observe the discipline of the Order, but despise the wholesome lessons of his superiors, and even the superior himself, let him remember that the thoughts of our hearts are known to God, and that, unless he repents in time, he will not escape the eternal torments of hell, wherein there is no order, but where everlasting horror dwells (*Jb* 10:22).

Endeavour, therefore, to avoid the terrible judgements of God by constantly doing his will in fear and righteousness, in order that God may keep you in holy religion, and that in his mercies he may preserve you from punishment in hell. God will abundantly reward those who are faithful in his service; for God gives great rewards for small services, eternal rewards for temporal services, as he himself has promised his disciples, who, having abandoned all they had, asked what should be their reward: "You shall receive a hundredfold, and shall possess life everlasting" (*Mt* 19:29).

With these words, he set out from the place he loved in service of the God he loved even more.

Norbert Chosen to Become
Archbishop of Magdeburg

Before leaving Prémontré, he confided the administration of the abbey to Hugh, his first disciple. Norbert and Count Theobald then started on their journey. On reaching the border of Germany they were met by the deputies of the Marquess of Crayburg, who brought news that Maud was seriously ill. Since Count Theobald was travelling with all his court, Norbert went on ahead to Regensburg to find out what was happening.

On his way there he had to pass through Spires, where Lothair, King of the Romans – later to be crowned Emperor in 1132 – was holding a diet. The news of Norbert's arrival soon spread and Lothair expressed his wish to see him.

There were also present officials from Magdeburg who had come to ask the Pope's legates and Lothair for a new archbishop, their last one having recently died.

The natural choice for this was Norbert. During a meeting of the assembled prelates, all present proclaimed him by acclamation as the new Archbishop of Magdeburg. The officials from Magdeburg rejoiced at this happy result.

Norbert, with tears in his eyes, entreated them not to confirm the election. The papal legates and Lothair made use of their authority to oblige him to yield. Norbert had to submit to God's will and was consecrated Archbishop of Magdeburg.

Norbert, now being unable to proceed to Regensburg, sent one of his disciples to see Maud, Theobald's future wife. Happily, she had recovered, and the two were married with the blessing of their good friend Norbert.

Spires was full of admiration for Norbert, and congratulated Magdeburg on the choice of such a holy and learned archbishop. Their admiration increased when they saw Norbert leaving the town barefooted and clothed in the white habit of the Order.

At a distance from his archiepiscopal city, he was met by the clergy and the principal inhabitants of his diocese, and amidst the acclamations of the crowd he was conducted to the bishop's palace. His dress was so mean and poor that the porter took him for a beggar and shut the door against him. Those present saw the porter's mistake and cried out, "He is our bishop." Norbert smiled and said to the porter, "Do not fear for you know me better than those who have raised such a one to this high dignity and who force me into the palace."

Norbert Defends the Rights of the Church and a Successor is Chosen for Prémontré

Norbert's first act was to do away with unnecessary grandeur. In doing so he followed his love of poverty and humility. His austerities were the same as those which he practised in the cloister; his palace was like a monastery. By his eloquence and good example, he caused a great reform of life both in the clergy and the laity of his diocese. Sadly, this was not without its troubles.

Knowing that a bishop is not only answerable for the souls of his flock, but also for the possessions of his church, he carefully examined the title deeds of his ecclesiastical property. He found that a considerable portion of church lands had fallen into possession of some powerful noblemen.

His first work was to collect whatever title deeds he could find and the history of such property. He then sent his commissioners to explain the result of his inquiry and to reclaim the patrimony of the church.

Some restored their ill-gotten church lands; others were unwilling to part with them and so became Norbert's greatest enemies. They called Norbert a miser, a hypocrite, a stranger, who was far too fond of money. Norbert, faithful to his sacred ministry, remained firm and determined to recover what belonged to the church and the people.

The archbishop behaved in the same principled way with those of the clergy who had openly broken their vows and who led double lives. He happily touched the hearts of many priests, but unfortunately, others became more obstinate in their rebellion and these he reluctantly threatened with the penalties of excommunication. With this he overcame most resistance and re-established the good reputation of the priesthood.

Norbert felt that his new episcopal duties did not allow him the ability to see to the interests of the Order in general, and of Prémontré in particular. He therefore resolved to have an Abbot General elected in his place, who would have the direction of the whole Order.

He asked his brethren to unite their prayers, acts of charity and penance for this intention. He asked some of his earliest and chief disciples to meet at Magdeburg to deliberate together on this matter.

God revealed to Norbert that he desired that Hugh, his first disciple, should take his place and that he would possess the spirit of the founder in the government of his Order.

And so Hugh was elected unanimously. Having received Norbert's blessing, Hugh was installed as Abbot of Prémontré and General of the whole Order.

His first act was to invoke a General Chapter. At this chapter meeting, it was decreed that the General, the abbots and the provosts should be elected for life and that the General Chapter should be the highest and supreme tribunal of the Order, to which the abbots and even the General should owe their obedience. The fast was changed from a perpetual one into one of seven months, but flesh meat was never allowed. Besides this, there were special rules made for the abbots, the priors and all the officials of the abbey. It was also decided that the General Chapter should meet each year at Prémontré on the feast of St Denis.

Norbert Establishes His Brethren in Magdeburg; Plots Against Norbert

Norbert wanted to see some of his brethren from Prémontré permanently established near him at Magdeburg. However, this idea met with general opposition especially from some of his clergy who were still unhappy at Norbert's reforms. Eventually he prevailed on the canons of St Mary's chapter to give up their church for his brethren.

When Norbert saw his cherished plans realised, he named Evermode, one of his faithful companions, as provost of the young community. This house soon became the centre of holy, learned and zealous missionaries who succeeded in reviving the faith in Saxony, where it had been darkened by superstitions and ignorance.

Norbert's reforming zeal did not please everyone. Some laymen and priests conspired against the energetic archbishop, even to making attempts on his life. They bribed a young cleric who went as a penitent on Maundy Thursday (12th April 1129) to the chapel were Norbert was hearing confessions. When the young man drew near, Norbert bade him stand still. Norbert then requested his attendants to take off the cleric's cloak and they found a large knife. When Norbert asked him why he had come to confession with a knife, the young man fell on his knees, confessed his intended crime and told the names of his fellow conspirators. To the great astonishment of all present, it was discovered that Atticus, Norbert's archdeacon, was amongst the conspirators. The virtuous archbishop only remarked that no one ought to be surprised to see those plots instigated by the archenemy, who, during that same sacred night (Holy Thursday), induced the Jews to plot against the life of Christ. He added that he should consider himself fortunate were he found worthy to have a share in the sacred Passion of Our Lord, especially on that sacred day.

The conspirators next persuaded a priest who resided in the archbishop's palace to make another attempt on the life of Norbert, this time at midnight, when the priests were going to the church to sing the office of matins. The priest hid himself in one of the dark passages and with his dagger struck the last person in the procession, thinking this was the archbishop. But it so happened that Norbert did not walk at the end of the procession, as he was accustomed to do, but amid his priests. The would-be assassin wounded and nearly killed a chaplain instead of the archbishop. The priest ran away and when the other priests pursued him, Norbert restrained them saying, "Let him escape and do not render evil for evil; he has done his worst and all that God permitted him to do."

No calumny or violence could make him forsake the
duties of his sacred ministry. One of Norbert's sayings
was, "Calumny is the test of a patient and generous heart
which bears with it rather than give up working for God."
Another was, "He who has God on his side is troubled at
nothing." These principles he truly lived out with joy.

This generous humility did not change the hearts of
his enemies. They now publicly declared that they would
no longer submit to a man who, they said, only sought
to harass his clergy by his harsh regulations and to rob
the rich for his own profit. They spread all kinds of false
rumours, and by their calumnies so excited the people
against Norbert that the slightest reason would be enough
to make them openly express their anger. Such a pretext
for this was soon found.

A Riot in Magdeburg and More Plots Against Norbert

A terrible crime had been committed in the cathedral of Magdeburg and so the archbishop wished to purify the cathedral according to the laws of the Church. He proposed to his chapter to have this done at once. Either from ignorance or from a spirit of opposition, the cathedral canons would not hear of having the ceremony performed. Norbert told them that he would not celebrate the Holy Sacrifice of the Mass if the cathedral remained in its state of profanation. He addressed his flock and explained to them what the Church ordered to be done on similar occasions.

Seeing, however, that the opposition was so very strong, the archbishop decided to perform the necessary ceremonies in private and purified the cathedral at night, being assisted in his functions by his two suffragans – the bishops of Havelberg and of Misnia – and by a small number of priests and clerics.

Meanwhile, some of the cathedral canons and those who sided with them, roused the inhabitants and spread the rumour that Norbert was breaking down and ransacking the altars and shrines. They lied saying that Norbert intended to remove all the treasures of the cathedral.

The rage of the people exploded; the service of purification had barely concluded when the cathedral was surrounded by a turbulent crowd. Their wild cries frightened all who were with Norbert, but he did not show any fear and wanted to confront the rioters. However, the suffragans and his assistant priests forced him to seek safety with them in the cathedral tower.

During the long hours of the night, the hostile crowd grew and grew. As dawn broke, some of those who had sworn to kill Norbert succeeded in scaling the tower. No sooner had Norbert seen them rush in with their drawn swords, than he went to meet them. "You seek but one person, behold here I am. But I ask of you not to touch those who are with me and who are innocent."

Norbert, who still wore his pontifical vestments, said these words with such calm and dignity, that the invaders fell on their knees and asked for pardon. They even offered their services to protect him against the attacks of the assailants and so, from being enemies, instantly became his protectors.

The head magistrate had in the meantime returned to Magdeburg and hearing what had occurred he ordered the crowd to disperse peacefully.

As to Norbert, he returned to the cathedral and celebrated a Mass of thanksgiving for the protection of God. From the foot of the altar he thus addressed those present, "See, those things which I have been accused of having broken and removed are still here whole and entire as they were before." He then commenced his Mass, rejoicing that he had been found worthy to suffer.

The calm was short lived, for his enemies again met to plot against the archbishop. They now made a strange agreement that for a certain number of days all should take a fixed quantity of wine, so that the murder which they had planned might be attributed to the effects of drunkenness.

When this came to the ears of the magistrates of the town, they advised Norbert to leave Magdeburg for a while. Norbert refused to go, and joyfully anticipated the hour when he should receive the crown of martyrdom.

When the day that the conspirators had agreed upon had arrived, with cries and shouts they rushed into the streets and made their way to the provostry of St Mary. Norbert inquired what the noise meant. He was told that there was a great crowd going to expel his religious from their monastery. At these words Norbert smiled and said, "They will not succeed, for that which the Heavenly Father has planted, cannot be destroyed by the hand of man."

His friends, however, insisted that he leave his palace. Norbert went to the Abbey of St John the Baptist, situated in a suburb of Magdeburg, where he stayed only long enough to arrange matters concerning his diocese. He then proceeded to a house of canons nearby, where he remained for a few days, continually asking God's pardon for his people.

Norbert Returns to Magdeburg

In a short time, the people of Magdeburg saw how badly they had been misled. At a public meeting, the whole town resolved to send some deputies to the Abbey of Petersburg, to entreat the archbishop to forgive them and to return to his flock.

Norbert received the deputies with the love of a father. He forgave them wholeheartedly. They had accused him of love of money, but he had only vindicated the rights of the Church. As to compensation, he would receive himself none, except their repentance.

The whole town now wished to make full amends for the injury done to the priesthood in the person of Norbert and went in procession to conduct their archbishop back to Magdeburg, where he was received in triumph.

The people could now see what a holy and zealous archbishop they had in Norbert. From this moment they became so firmly and generously attached to him that the calumnies of Atticus and his associates could no longer separate the flock from their pastor. All this occurred during the third year of Norbert's episcopate.

During the next five years that Norbert occupied the see of Magdeburg, says his first biographer, he was day by day engaged in the work of his sacred ministry. He was "an angel at the altar, a father in the confessional, another St John the Baptist in the pulpit."

Yet Norbert had more trials to face; these were difficult times. At that time, Rome was governed by an antipope, Peter di Leone, who had assumed the name of Anacletus.

Norbert Opposes Anacletus

Peter di Leone (also known as Pierleoni) was the grandson of a convert who, on his conversion to Christianity, had taken the name of Leo in memory of Pope Leo IX. The influence which his family had in Rome was great and in their desire for power they destined Peter for the highest honours in the Church.

Peter, having completed his course of studies at Paris, became a monk at Cluny. Pope Calixtus II recalled him to Rome and promoted him to the dignity of cardinal.

It was this same Cardinal Peter di Leone who, together with Cardinal Gregory Papareschi de Angelis, had approved of the Order of Prémontré in 1124.

At the death of Pope Honorius II on the 14th February 1130, both these cardinals were elected to succeed him. Peter di Leone, by his riches and power, had bribed several cardinals and was elected under the name Anacletus. Other members of the Sacred College, foreseeing the success of Peter's intrigues, had already elected Cardinal Gregory under the title of Innocent II.

The followers of Innocent and Anacletus soon came to open hostilities. The Roman troops and the mob paid by

Anacletus marched against Innocent, who first took refuge in the house of the Frangipani, and afterwards embarked secretly on the Tiber, with all his cardinals, and arrived at Pisa.

Anacletus, now master of Rome, wrote to Lothair and to other sovereigns, announcing his election to the pontifical throne. The bishop sent to bring the letter to Lothair also had one for Norbert. In this letter, Anacletus spoke in flattering terms of Norbert and his Order. He now asked Norbert to follow him and to use his great influence with Lothair to persuade him to accept Anacletus as pope. Norbert, who had already been informed of the nullity of Peter di Leone's election, received these letters with contempt and replied that far from using his influence in his favour, he would use it against Anacletus.

Anacletus was disappointed at this reply. He changed his tactics and used the investigation of a charge which Atticus, the former archdeacon of Magdeburg, had brought against Norbert in order to put pressure on Norbert to come over to his side.

The Rightful Pope

Atticus was still the leading spirit in the faction at Magdeburg against Norbert. Having repeatedly been found guilty of injustices in the execution of his office, he had been dismissed from his office and had been suspended by the archbishop. Against this judgement, Atticus had appealed to the antipope and had gone to Rome to defend his cause.

Anacletus therefore wrote to Norbert and instructed the Archbishop of Magdeburg to appear before him, but he added that it was less to judge him than to have the pleasure of seeing again an old friend.

Norbert treated this citation with silent contempt. The antipope now ordered the archbishop to re-establish Atticus in his former dignity and commanded him a second time to Rome. Norbert took no notice of this order and the antipope finally passed sentence of excommunication against him.

Whilst all this was taking place, Norbert was at the Council of Rheims, where his presence was the cause of great consolation to Pope Innocent II in his exile. Norbert presented him letters from Lothair who assured His Holiness of his allegiance and moreover promised him the aid of his army to expel Anacletus from the pontifical throne.

At the close of the council, the Pope left Rheims and proceeded to Laon. Norbert accompanied him, as he had an earnest desire to revisit his dear Prémontré. The arrival of Norbert at Prémontré was the occasion of great joy for both Norbert and his brothers at Prémontré.

The sovereign pontiff, accompanied by his prelates, also visited. The Pope's good impression was now confirmed by what he witnessed: how men of great learning practised the austerities of poverty and religious discipline; how five hundred religious lived together as brethren, united by the same spirit and working for the same end; and how they all observed the exercises of the contemplative life and fulfilled the priestly functions of the active ministry. The virtues of these fervent religious so edified Innocent II that he again confirmed, as sovereign pontiff, the Order which he had already confirmed as legate of Pope Honorius.

As much as Norbert desired to remain longer with his brethren at Prémontré, the Pope asked him to return to Germany, so that he might speak with Lothair. Norbert did as the Pope had asked and he found Lothair still faithful to his promise to send an army to Rome.

Norbert Accompanies the Emperor to Rome to Restore the Rightful Pope

Lothair had gathered an army of about four thousand men to march on Rome and restore Pope Innocent to the papal throne. He asked Norbert to accompany him and appointed him Chancellor of the Holy Roman Empire.

Lothair left Augsburg with his troops and continued his march by way of Milan and then on to Pisa, where Pope Innocent II, St Bernard of Clairvaux and many prelates of the Church awaited the Emperor and his army. Here Pope Innocent II and Lothair decided that the troops should continue their march by land and that the Pope should proceed by sea.

Soon after, Peter di Leone was struck with panic when he heard that Lothair had encamped his army at a place called San Valentino and that Innocent II had arrived at Viterbo. He sent an embassy to Lothair in order to gain time and endeavoured to win him over to his cause, but the ambassadors failed in their mission. Facing disaster, Peter di Leone devised one more intrigue which was to appeal to Lothair to decide between him and his opponent.

Lothair agreed to do so and, acting on the advice of Norbert and other prelates, he decided that Pope Innocent II was indeed the true and legitimate Pope.

Angered at this decision, Peter di Leone refused to submit to it and appealed to a General Council. At once, Lothair marched his army to Rome. Since he met with no opposition in the city of Rome, his army encamped on the Aventine Hill, near the church of St Sabina, while the Pope was enthroned in the Lateran.

As for the antipope, he did not try to resist the imperial army, but he hid in the castle of Sant'Angelo with his adherents. They had surrounded the area around St Peter's with fortifications and barricades.

The Alliance of Pope Innocent and Lothair

Anacletus perceived that his cause would be ended if Lothair were to be crowned Emperor by Pope Innocent II. The adherents of the antipope accordingly stirred up the people of Rome the day before the coronation. This was all in vain for, on account of this disturbance, the ceremony took place in the Lateran Basilica instead of at St Peter's.

By this solemn act, the two powers were consolidated anew in the eyes of the world. It was also on this occasion that Pope Innocent II gave to Norbert the dignity of Primate of Germany.

The author of the first manuscript life of St Norbert having chronicled these events, goes on to describe what happened next:

> Lothair, being now crowned Emperor, had the audacity to ask of the Pope to grant him, for the honour of the Empire and the stability of the compact which he had made with him, the privilege of investiture, that is, the liberty of the churches. The Pope seemed inclined to grant this request and none even of the Bishops spoke against this abuse, until Norbert arose in their midst and exclaimed in the presence of the Emperor and his officer, 'What do you mean to do, O Father? To whom do you deliver up the sheep committed to your care, to be torn to pieces? You have received the Church in freedom; will you reduce her now to slavery? The Chair of Peter demands the works of Peter. I have indeed promised obedience to Blessed Peter and to you in the name of Christ; but if you do what is now asked of you, behold I gainsay you in the face of the whole church.' The determination of Norbert meant that the Emperor no longer urged his unreasonable request, nor did the Pope yield to him. For the Emperor feared God and he loved Norbert as a man sent from heaven.

Lothair left Rome with his troops and recrossed the Alps. Norbert, who had suffered much from the Italian climate and was now very ill, accompanied the Emperor back to Germany.

The Death and Burial of Norbert

The health of Norbert was now growing weaker and the archbishop was continually subject to acute bodily sufferings, caused by the difficulties of the journey and his austere mortifications. Norbert reached Magdeburg exhausted by his infirmities and the length of the journey.

With sufferings and full of good works, Norbert was now ready for heaven, but God, who had given him so many triumphs during his life, reserved for him another triumph before his death.

The inhabitants of Magdeburg rejoiced to see their beloved archbishop and in their confidence in his saintly power to work miracles they laid at his feet the corpses of three men.

The saint was touched by their tears. Having invoked Almighty God to restore them to life, and bending over their bodies, he commanded life to return to them. His prayer was granted, for the three men rose up and walked, and Norbert restored them to their relatives.

As his illness increased, he received with tender devotion the last sacraments of the Church. Finally, he gave his last blessing to his diocese, to his spiritual children, and to his servants, and casting his eyes towards heaven, he peacefully expired in the Lord on the Wednesday after Pentecost, which fell in that year, 1134, on the 6th June, at the age of fifty-four years. Nineteen of these years he had spent in penance, eighteen in the labours of his apostolic zeal, and eight in his episcopal duties.

Immediately after his death Norbert, clad in white and holding an olive branch in his hands, appeared to a religious of the Order, who was working at one of the granges belonging to the Abbey of Prémontré. The brother, astonished at the vision, asked him where he came from and where he was going. To this Norbert replied that he came from heaven, and that he was going to transplant the green olive branch in the house of his poverty. "The house of poverty" was the name Norbert loved to call the Abbey of Prémontré. It was afterwards found that this apparition had taken place on the very day and at the very hour that Norbert had died at Magdeburg.

Norbert's Place of Burial

Meanwhile, in Magdeburg, following his death, the canons of the cathedral demanded that the body of their Archbishop should be buried in the cathedral. On the other hand, the Norbertine canons of St Mary's naturally wished that their saintly founder should rest in the church of his children.

As the two could not agree, they determined to have this question decided by the Emperor. Eventually, the Emperor sent word that Norbert should be buried with his sons at St Mary's.

Whilst they awaited the Emperor's decision, the body lay unburied, exposed to the veneration of the public, and was carried each day in turn to one of the city churches. Though the weather was excessively hot for June, the body preserved its freshness of colour, as if he were not dead, but sleeping. The beautiful odour which came from the body manifested the glory of this temple of the Holy Spirit.

This miracle has continued ever since, even when, at the time of the Reformation, the Norbertine canons had been expelled from St Mary's and the tomb had fallen into the hands of Lutherans. This odour caused the Lutheran pastor of St Mary's to try and open the tomb. His sacrilegious hand was held back, and the impious reformer was struck dead on the spot.

Miracles at Norbert's Shrine and the Removal of His Relics to Prague

The tomb of Norbert became famous throughout all Saxony, on account of the numerous miracles, and of the extraordinary graces obtained through the intercession of the holy archbishop. It was evident that the holiness of Norbert was proclaimed by the voice of the people and that he had obtained the following of a saint. It was Pope Gregory XIII who extended his cultus to the whole Church and fixed his feast on the 6th June.

The burial place of Norbert had much to suffer during the time of the Reformation – the Norbertine canons were expelled, and the Lutherans took possession of their church and consequently of the tomb of Norbert. The whole Order lamented to see the relics of their holy founder in the hands of these 'reformers', to whom nothing was sacred. John Lohelius, Abbot of Strahov, and afterwards Archbishop of Prague, and John de Pruetis, Abbot General of Prémontré, united in their endeavours to obtain possession of the precious relics. Eventually, it was Gaspar von Questenberg, who had succeeded John Lohelius in the abbatial dignity of Strahov, who pleaded with Ferdinand II, Emperor of

Germany, who then wrote to his civil and military officials in the district of Magdeburg to instruct them to allow the Abbot of Strahov to retrieve the relics.

The Abbot of Strahov proceeded, on the 3rd December 1626, to inspect the tomb and its sacred contents. He gave a description of the body, which was still intact, and of the sacred vestments in which the saint had been buried nearly five hundred years before.

The ecclesiastical and civil authorities of Bohemia had proclaimed Norbert as one of the chosen protectors, or patron saints, of the kingdom, and had arranged the order of ceremonies to be observed during the festivities of the translation of the relics which began on 2nd May 1627.

During this solemn procession to Prague, a great number of miracles were recorded through the intercession of Norbert. The Chancellery of Bohemia preserves the testimony of six hundred Protestants who were reconciled to the Catholic Church during this solemn procession.

Prayer to St Norbert

The abbot and canons of the Abbey of Strahov are still the guardians of the relics of our holy founder. In his honour, and before his shrine, they daily sing the following antiphon with verse and prayer:

This saint is a vessel of election filled with the Holy Spirit; this is Norbert, the great friend of God; he is a valiant champion, who fought with the serpent of old; he is an angel of peace, a herald of penance, powerful in words and deeds, by his miracles and his prophecies. Let us, his children, approach him, our Father; let us, his clients, approach him, our Patron Saint. Let us with a supplicant voice pray to him, and say: O saint of God, O friend of the Spouse, O Norbert, our Father and Guardian, the glory of our Order, pray to the Lord for us, make Him propitious unto us. Hear us, O hear us, St Norbert! Make those whom thou hast deemed worthy to be called thy Sons ever feel the benefit of thy powerful intercession.

V. The Lord keepeth all the bones of the just
R. Not one of them shall be broken

Let us pray

O God, who art glorious in thy saints, and through their intercession canst be pacified, we beseech thee to protect this place which thou has deigned to honour with the venerable relics of St Norbert, who is under thee our Father, and also to protect all those who dwell in it, together with our King and his kingdom, and to preserve them through his guardianship from all evil and all enemies, through our Lord Jesus Christ. Amen.

Norbertines in England

Only twenty-two years after the foundation of the Order in 1121, the White Canons (as we became known in England) came to England to establish the first Norbertine abbey at Newhouse, in Lincolnshire. Between 1143 and the Dissolution of the Monasteries under Henry VIII, our Order in England firmly established itself as part of the nation's monastic and parochial life. Some thirty-three abbeys and priories are recorded during this period and then, as now, the main occupation of the Norbertine canons was prayer and apostolate in the parishes which depended on the canons for their pastors.

Many other functions were fulfilled by our pre-Reformation confrères. In 1200, the Abbot of Torre (Devon) was appointed King John's representative at the Papal Curia. In 1207, the Abbot of St Radegmund (Kent) was sent as royal ambassador to Count William of Holland. Henry IV used the services of the Abbot of Alnwick (Northumberland) to negotiate with the Scottish Earl of March in 1400. The Abbot of Tichfield (Hampshire) had responsibilities for the building of Porchester Castle. England's Treasurer in 1264 was a Norbertine prior, while a certain Brother Thomas was a trusted advisor to Henry III.

A few early Norbertines attained distinction in intellectual and ecclesiastical fields. Many pre-Reformation abbots held law degrees from either Oxford or Cambridge. Abbot Makerell took degrees at both Cambridge and Frieburg and was appointed suffragan bishop in the dioceses of York and Lincoln. Fr Thomas Wygenhall, of the Abbey of West Dereham, wrote treatises on law and moral theology. "Richard the Premonstratensian" wrote a number of theological works, while Adam the Scot, born in the twelfth century and known to have been a member of the community at Dryburgh, was renowned both as a preacher and a writer throughout Europe.

By far the most important work of the Order before the Reformation was to be found in the parishes. In the fourteenth century the Norbertines had some 150 parishes in England. The Order's contribution to the life of the Church in England, Wales and Scotland is witnessed to by the number of priests who were sent to work in diocesan parishes without, however, losing contact with the abbey or priory to which they belonged. These close links with the parochial apostolate would be characteristic of the Order when it returned to England in 1872 after the centuries of post-Reformation exile.

The return of the White Canons to England is the responsibility of two of the great abbeys of our Order, the

Abbey of Tongerlo in Belgium (founded parishes in the north of England) and the Abbey of Frigolet in France (opened houses in Farnborough and Storrington).

At the request of local Catholics, the Abbot of Tongerlo dispatched Fr Martin Geudens to Crowle in Lincolnshire in 1872. This mission soon grew and attracted the first English vocations to the Norbertines since the Reformation.

In 1889, Norbertines went to Manchester where they lived and worked at Corpus Christi in Miles Platting. It was there that our present canonry became an independent priory in 2004. The community then transferred to Chelmsford in 2008. We are the first Norbertine community to live in Essex for over 470 years. We serve two busy parishes in the city and are also involved in a wide variety of apostolates, both near and far. These apostolates reflect the active and contemplative nature of our life as Norbertines.

For over nine hundred years, our Order has striven to proclaim the gospel of Jesus Christ and work tirelessly for the salvation of souls. We do this through the "communio" we share, lived out by singing the praise of God in the Holy Mass and Divine Office; in lifting high the Blessed Sacrament above all the errors and miseries of the world; by loving our Blessed Mother; in a zeal for souls; and in a life of sacrifice and penance.

If you feel called to serve God as a Norbertine in our community, or would like further information on our life and work, please visit our website: *www.norbertines.org.uk* or email us: *community@ norbertines.org.uk*